The discipline of writing something down is the first step toward making it happen.

-Lee Iacocca

Contents

Overvew

Hello. I am glad you took the first step towards rebuilding your credit. Many people do not realize exactly how important a good credit profile is, or that a bad credit history could easily cost you four hundred thousand dollars in your lifetime[1]. I certainly don't have that kind of money to just throw away.

I wrote this book after years of lying to myself, saying my credit did not matter since I could always pay in cash or use my debit card. After a friend directed me towards a video about credit on YouTube I felt very foolish. Not only did I have bad credit, but the way I was handling it would never help at all.

My entire view about credit cards and credit in general now has changed, and so has the way I use them. Today I intentionally use my credit cards as much as possible.

Why did I take the time to write this book? Well, everything I have learned on my quest to better credit scores has taught me three things.

---

[1] https://lifehacker.com/how-much-does-a-bad-credit-score-really-cost-you-1847896252

First, whether the result is from action or inaction my credit mess is my own fault. Which means I am the one that must now fix it. Next is the cool part, which is an important truth. There is nothing a credit repair company or law firm can do to fix a person's credit that the person cannot do themselves[2]. Nothing.

Ignore the advertisements about cloud software and "guaranteed results" credit repair law firms. Paying them is like paying for someone to tell you to tie your own shoes. The only advantage they had over you, until now, is that they already know the information contained in this book. Soon, you will as well. Finally comes the somewhat unpleasant truth. Credit scores are just a numerical summary of your credit habits, the history of which is detailed in your credit reports. Credit history builds over time, so do not expect your scores to jump overnight. You can, however, see very positive results in a little as five months.

Today I look at my credit scores only as a gauge of my credit health. Just like my heartbeat and blood pressure, they will vary slightly with my recent activities. The overall average, however, tells me if I am on the right track. I look at my credit history the same way a doctor views a patient's medical history. Simple changes in behavior, over time, will make a huge difference in both.

---

[2] https://consumer.ftc.gov/articles /fixing-your-credit-faqs

In this book we briefly look at the origins of credit reporting. We examine why it became necessary then uncover how the three largest credit reporting agencies each began.

Understanding the intended purpose of the credit reporting companies is paramount to deciphering your credit reports. You will see why these companies actually prefer to include negative information – even if it is incorrect.

Credit reporting all started over one hundred years ago.

History of Credit Reporting

Before attempting to negotiate with the credit reporting agencies, it is worthwhile to know exactly what it is that they do, and why they even exist. We will now step through a quick summary outlining the history of credit reports and the companies that produce them.

Initially, credit reporting was a very simple method for shopkeepers to secure loans. The business owners would ask well respected neighbors to vouch for them, insisting that they would readily repay their debts. In cities with larger populations, lenders would have to rely on rumor mills to try and weed out who the risky borrowers might be. Credit was mainly for businesses at that time.

In the early 1800s the sheer number of different businesses made it very difficult for lenders to decide credit worthiness in a timely manner. Also, new laws would soon permit the declaration of bankruptcy. This multiplied the risk to lenders since it increased the chances of them losing money with uncollectible debts. Trivial methods were employed to simplify the evaluation of risks with business loans, most of which were unsuccessful.

In 1841 a merchant named Lewis Tappan created an entity called the Mercantile Agency. Its purpose was to once and for all make it easier to assess the risks presented by potential debtors, and to summarize both their assets and their character. Four years prior there was an economic depression. Merchants had extended far more credit than was collectible and the result was insurmountable losses for most lenders.

Bad debt was extremely costly and wiped out several lenders. That specific problem is what the entities that evolved to become the credit reporting agencies today were created to solve.

In 1899 the Retail Credit company was created in Atlanta by two brothers named Cator Woolford and Guy Woolford. Their method of gathering data began with door-to-door visits, asking merchants about their customers and recording the details they were provided.

The two men created their own system of notations to describe the customers and their payment habits, which was easy to understand. They would go on to publish all their findings in "The Merchant's Guide" which they sold for $25 each copy. There was a lot of money to be made from making this valuable information available, and they even offered individual credit reports.

Cator had experience working for a bank and Guy was a lawyer, so their backgrounds gave their reports great credibility.

By 1965 their creation, the Retail Credit Company, had expanded so much that it went public. But it soon came under scrutiny of the Federal Trade Commission (FTC). In 1971 after the Fair Credit Reporting Act was signed into law, the Retail Credit Company was initially identified as a frequent violator. Eventually, in 1979 the Retail Credit Company officially changed its name to Equifax, the name it continues using today.

Back in 1897 a man named Jim Chilton started what would become one of the first credit reporting companies in the United States. He worked at his uncle's law firm which put him in contact with many local merchants plagued by the same problem, which was no longer personally knowing most of the customers to which they extended credit. Customers would often disappear without paying their debts and show up elsewhere with completely different identities.

After gathering information from several merchants Jim recorded and organized the scattered customer information, then established the Merchant's Credit Association. It provided every subscriber with an annual directory that detailed the credit worthiness of many potential customers.

The Merchant's Credit Association began listing not only good credit risks but also those it identified as bad, and convinced merchants to privately share the information with each other. By 1953 their methods of retrieving physical index cards from file cabinets to access credit information had become rather burdensome. A company called TRW was founded that year, and after it entered the industry in 1968, years later TRW would use electronic systems to quickly share credit data.

In the 1980s, the use of credit cards in the United States had rapidly multiplied, and lenders needed to make decisions far more quickly and accurately. TRW used statisticians to create summary credit scoring models in addition to providing business and real estate information. In 1996 TRW was sold and the name of the company was changed to Experian.

TransUnion was created as a parent holding company for another entity in 1968, which then acquired the Credit Bureau of Cook County (CBCC). CBCC already managed the records for more than three and a half million consumers, but it did so by using about four hundred file cabinets that were seven drawers tall. Obviously, continuing to manage information this way would be much too slow.

TransUnion became the first credit reporting company that switched from paper records to automated tape-to-disc transfer. By 1988

TransUnion was operating nationwide and had expanded its offerings to business-to-business services and data analytics. By the year 2002 TransUnion purchased TrueCredit.com which is how it entered the direct-to-consumer market, where customers can now access their credit report details online.

Equifax, Experian and TransUnion exist to collect and share data about prospective borrowers (customers) to the lenders who desperately need the information. Credit reporting is big business, and the accuracy of the data is what makes it valuable. Except keeping inaccurate data can also be valuable. But how? The concept is terribly simple.

Lenders would often see their businesses fail after giving the benefit of doubt to customers who later proved unreliable. Credit reporting agencies protected these companies from losses not by offering guarantees about good customers, but by collecting negative information about bad ones. Whichever agency had collected the most negative details about customers was naturally considered the most thorough, making their data most reliable - so their credit reports were the most valuable. Bad credit reports meant higher risk, so higher fees and interest rates could be charged. Bad credit reports became a very valuable to lenders. Credit reporting is big business.

Can you see how this became a problem? The agencies once searched for any kind of negative personal information unrelated to credit that could be used to deem customers undesirable. Racism and other factors could be hidden within their credit scoring models, to give blatant discrimination the appearance of legitimacy. Fairness in credit reporting did not apply to everyone.

The Fair Credit Reporting Act (FCRA) was passed into law in 1970. Originally the actual title read "An Act to amend the Federal Deposit Insurance Act to require insured banks to maintain certain records, to require that certain transactions in United States currency be reported to the Department of the Treasury, and for other purposes." Yeah. The FCRA resulted from frustration of lawmakers with individuals being powerless to remove errors from their credit reports. It was enacted to help shield consumers from willful or negligent inclusion of errors. Now there can be no more secret databases used to make decisions about a person's life, individuals can review and challenge their credit record details and outdated information must expire[3].

A backdoor of sorts does exist that works to the advantage of the credit reporting companies. Since anyone can review their credit reports each year for free, some of the burden is lifted from the

____

[3] https://en.wikipedia.org/wiki/Fair_Credit_Reporting_Act

agencies concerning incorrect negative information. If you do not review your credit reports and challenge any details, they reason, everything in them must be correct.

People with unfavorable credit reports are a gold mine for credit issuers. Poor credit scores are ample justification for charging extremely high interest rates, which means the creditors will earn much more money than from those with great scores.

Getting Your Credit Reports

To address your credit issues, you need to first find out exactly what they are. As we have already learned, the three primary companies that generate credit reports and track history are Equifax, Experian, and TransUnion. A misnomer about each of these is that they are government agencies. They are not, and each one instead remains a for profit company.

Companies must follow specific rules and when they do not abide by them, they can each be held liable and sued. The set of rules that specifically governs the credit reporting agencies is called the Fair Credit Reporting Act [15 U.S.C § 1681][4]. I suggest that you download a copy of this document, browse the table of contents therein and specifically review sections 609 through 612.

Once you read and understand the rules governing the credit reporting agencies, you should take a bow. Without any certificate or having to

---

[4] https://www.ftc.gov/system/files/documents/statutes/fair-credit-reporting-act/545a_fair-credit-reporting-act-0918.pdf

become a "hero" you will have the full details you need to successfully tackle issues with your credit reports. You can read the FCRA at your leisure since I do present the most important details relevant to credit repair in this book.

To begin, you should know how much it will cost to obtain your credit reports. That is covered in section 612 of the FCRA as follows:

§ 612. Charges for certain disclosures [15 U.S.C. § 1681j] See also 16 CFR Part 610 69 Fed. Reg. 35467 (06/24/04) 75 Fed. Reg. 9726 (03/03/10)

(a) Free Annual Disclosure (1) Nationwide Consumer Reporting Agencies (A) In general. All consumer reporting agencies described in subsections (p) and (w) of section 603 shall make all disclosures pursuant to section 609 once during any 12-month period upon request of the consumer and without charge to the consumer. (B) Centralized source. Subparagraph (A) shall apply with respect to a consumer reporting agency described in section 603(p) only if the request from the consumer is made using the centralized source established for such purpose in accordance with section 211(c) of the Fair and Accurate Credit Transactions Act of 2003.

The F.C.R.A. requires (not so plainly) that every consumer like you and I can get a free credit report from each agency once every twelve months. And there is a centralized source that was established for this purpose. The designated website covers all three credit reporting agencies, and the address is AnnualCreditReport.com. As the website details prominently under its title graphic, it is "The only source for your free credit reports. Authorized by Federal law".

If you have not yet obtained your credit reports, you should certainly do so. People have suggested various strategies concerning whether a person should get all their credit reports at once or stagger them so they can see changes while working through issues in each. Here is the correct answer.

Get all three credit reports immediately.

Time is the one thing you should not waste while working to fix your credit. Simple, right? And how about this one fact that answers the question precisely. The credit reporting companies are independent of each other, so changes made at one have no effect on the other two. You can spend weeks disputing details at Experian, but there will be absolutely no changes at TransUnion or Equifax as a result. Get all three of your credit reports right away.

Securing Your Personal Information

Each of your credit reports will likely span several pages. A good strategy to use when reviewing them is to begin with the personal information section.

In each of my reports I found many errors concerning my identity without much effort. Incorrectly spelled and wholly fictitious but similar sounding names, incorrect and incomplete birthdates and incorrect addresses were all there. I thought a good first step would be to write letters to each company demanding the false information be deleted.

Not so fast.

Before anything, you should scrub your personal information from each of the "people finder" sites. Like it or not, those very sites help facilitate identity theft, and are a treasure for people looking to defraud others. To request your personal information be removed from these sites you must complete a request to "Opt-out" of their personal information reporting.

There are several of these sites that exist solely to peddle your personal information, so you should opt-out of each one of them. A good starting point for personal data removal is LexisNexis (https://optout.lexisnexis.com). Unfortunately, the opt-out process with the many other data brokers and requesting removal is not always as straight forward.

A great site for helping to scrub your personal information from the internet is called DeleteMe, and although they will remove you from the data brokers for a fee, they do provide an excellent set of opt-out guides so you can do it yourself. Their link is:

https://joindeleteme.com/help/diy-free-opt-out-guide

At the very least you should opt-out of Spokeo, Mylife, Radaris, Whitepages, Intelius and BeenVerified which have convenient links on the page. But do not stop there. You can easily spend hours removing your personal data from other sites (more than fifty). I recommend it. DeleteMe has an extended list of opt-out links with instructions on how to request removal from each one for free. Here is the link:

https://joindeleteme.com/help/deleteme-help-topics/opt-out-guide/

Perhaps you never considered the importance of privacy before, especially as it relates to your credit report. I personally had not either, but I was alarmed by the sheer number of sites readily listing my personal information. These sites would not exist if there were no market for the data, so it is best to remove your personal information. Many people have been victims of identity theft without ever realizing it, until after reviewing their credit reports.

One comforting detail is that several of these data broker sites rely upon the others to gather information. This means that after following the procedure to opt-out of about twenty of them you may have eliminated ninety-five percent of the problem. How much time you devote to protecting your privacy is up to you, but secured personal information is an important part of accurate credit reporting.

With the opt-out process completed, you should next address any errors regarding your personal information contained in your credit reports. Since you often will need documents to prove your identity, here is a tip. I saved myself time by arranging on my scanner my driver license, Social Security card and a mailing from my medical insurance company that demonstrates my address. I scanned them and saved the single page as a pdf (portable document format created by adobe) file. Every time I need to send proof of identity, I simply print the file and attach the sheet with my correspondence.

Identifying incorrect details in the personal information section of each credit report is easy. Disputing them is also straightforward.

I prefer to send dispute letters, via certified mail, which is exactly how I got the false data deleted. Concerning errors with your personal information, though, each credit reporting company will let you dispute selected details of your personal online. My advice is to use whichever method you choose. But do not ever use online dispute methods for anything other than removing incorrect personal information!

Here is an example of a letter that I sent to Equifax (my personal name and address has been fictionalized):

August 8, 2022

John Q Smith
123 Main Street FL 2
Hometown, NJ 12345

Equifax Information Services LLC
P.O. Box 740256
Atlanta, GA 30348

To whom it may concern:

I am contacting you to remove disputed personal information and account details on file with your company, in accordance with 15 U.S.C. § 1681i , §611 a(1)-a(5). My correct information is detailed above and on the attached proof of identity documents. Listed below are the incorrect entries I did see on my

Credit Report. Please remove these entries and related inaccurate records.

For validation I have included proof of address and Identity.

I **do not** consent to have any telephone numbers listed on my report.

INCORRECT NAME:

I WAS NEVER FORMERLY KNOWN AS "JAMESQSMITH". SUCH NAME IS FRADULENT – IT AND ALL REFERENCES TO IT MUST BE REMOVED FROM MY CREDT REPORT AND RELATED RECORDS.

INCORRECT ADDRESSES:

108 Second St, Faketown, NJ 56789
202 Fooled Again Blvd, Faketown, NJ 56789

Thank you for your prompt attention to this matter.

Sincerely,

John Q Smith

Enclosures:

Driver License
SSN Card
Insurance Mailing

The format is very simple, and the letter gets quickly to the point. It also includes very important details which I am sure you observed. As promised, here are the excerpts from the FCRA that the example letter references:

§ 611. Procedure in case of disputed accuracy [15 U.S.C. § 1681i]

(a) Reinvestigations of Disputed Information

(1) Reinvestigation Required

(A) In general. Subject to subsection (f), and except as provided in subsection (g) if the completeness or accuracy of any item of information contained in a consumer's file at a consumer reporting agency is disputed by the consumer and the consumer notifies the agency directly, or indirectly through a reseller, of such dispute, the agency shall, free of charge, conduct a reasonable reinvestigation to determine whether the disputed information is inaccurate and record the current status of the disputed information, or delete the item from the file in accordance with paragraph (5), before the end of the 30-day period beginning on the date on which the agency receives the notice of the dispute from the consumer or reseller.

(B) Extension of period to reinvestigate. Except as provided in subparagraph (c), the 30-day period described in subparagraph (A) may be extended for not more than 15 additional days if the consumer reporting agency receives information from the consumer during that 30-day period that is relevant to the reinvestigation.

(C) Limitations on extension of period to reinvestigate. Subparagraph (B) shall not apply to any reinvestigation in which, during the 30-day period described in subparagraph (A), the information that is the subject of the reinvestigation is found to be inaccurate or incomplete or the consumer reporting agency determines that the information cannot be verified.

(2) Prompt Notice of Dispute to Furnisher of Information

(A) In general. Before the expiration of the 5-business-day period beginning on the date on which a consumer reporting agency receives notice of a dispute from any consumer or a reseller in accordance with paragraph (1), the agency shall provide notification of the dispute to any person who provided any item of information in dispute, at the address and in the manner established with the person. The notice shall include all relevant information regarding the dispute that the agency has received from the consumer or reseller.

(B) Provision of other information. The consumer reporting agency shall promptly provide to the person who provided the information in dispute all relevant information regarding the dispute that is received by the agency from the consumer or the reseller after the period referred to in subparagraph (A) and before the end of the period referred to in paragraph (1)(A).

(3) Determination That Dispute Is Frivolous or Irrelevant

(A) In general. Notwithstanding paragraph (1), a consumer reporting agency may terminate a reinvestigation of information disputed by a consumer under that paragraph if the agency reasonably determines that the dispute by the consumer is frivolous or irrelevant, including by reason of a failure by a consumer to provide sufficient information to investigate the disputed information.

(B) Notice of determination. Upon making any determination in accordance with subparagraph (A) that a dispute is frivolous or irrelevant, a consumer reporting agency shall notify the consumer of such determination not later than 5 business days after making such determination, by mail or, if authorized by the consumer for that purpose, by any other means available to the agency.

(C) Contents of notice. A notice under subparagraph (B) shall include

(i) the reasons for the determination under subparagraph (A); and

(ii) identification of any information required to investigate the disputed information, which may consist of a standardized form describing the general nature of such information.

(4) Consideration of consumer information.

In conducting any reinvestigation under paragraph (1) with respect to disputed information in the file of any consumer, the consumer reporting agency shall review and consider all relevant information submitted by the consumer in the period described in paragraph (1)(A) with respect to such disputed information.

(5) Treatment of Inaccurate or Unverifiable Information

(A) In general. If, after any reinvestigation under paragraph (1) of any information disputed by a consumer, an item of the information is found to be inaccurate or incomplete or cannot be verified, the consumer reporting agency shall –

(i) promptly delete that item of information from the file of the consumer, or modify that item of information, as appropriate, based on the results of the reinvestigation; and

(ii) promptly notify the furnisher of that information that the information has been modified or deleted from the file of the consumer.

(B) Requirements Relating to Reinsertion of Previously Deleted Material

(i) Certification of accuracy of information. If any information is deleted from a consumer's file pursuant to subparagraph (A), the information may not be reinserted in the file by the consumer reporting agency unless the person who furnishes the information certifies that the information is complete and accurate.

(ii) Notice to consumer. If any information that has been deleted from a consumer's file pursuant to subparagraph (A) is reinserted in the file, the consumer reporting agency shall notify the consumer of the reinsertion in writing not later than 5 business days after the reinsertion or, if authorized by the consumer for that purpose, by any other means available to the agency.

(iii) Additional information. As part of, or in addition to, the notice under clause (ii), a consumer reporting agency shall provide to a consumer in writing not later than 5 business days after the date of the reinsertion

    (I)a statement that the disputed information has been reinserted;

    (II) the business name and address of any furnisher of information contacted and the telephone number of such furnisher, if reasonably available, or of any furnisher of information that contacted the consumer reporting agency, in connection with the reinsertion of such information; and

(III) a notice that the consumer has the right to add a statement to the consumer's file disputing the accuracy or completeness of the disputed information.

(C) Procedures to prevent reappearance. A consumer reporting agency shall maintain reasonable procedures designed to prevent the reappearance in a consumer's file, and in consumer reports on the consumer, of information that is deleted pursuant to this paragraph (other than information that is reinserted in accordance with subparagraph (B)(i)).

D) Automated reinvestigation system. Any consumer reporting agency that compiles and maintains files on consumers on a nationwide basis shall implement an automated system through which furnishers of information to that consumer reporting agency may report the results of a reinvestigation that finds incomplete or inaccurate information in a consumer's file to other such consumer reporting agencies.

I agree that this is a lot to read. I decided to include it here rather than simply direct you to the link for it on the website of the Federal Trade Commission[5]. As you can see, there are specific steps that Equifax, Experian, and TransUnion must all follow to process disputes once they are submitted. Read it several times because there is certainly more to it than meets the eye.

Hopefully you noticed 15 U.S.C. § 1681i, §611 a(3) Determination That Dispute Is Frivolous or Irrelevant. This section is extremely important, and you should consider it to be both instructional and a warning.

Never submit a dispute concerning personal information that simply reads "it isn't me" or "I don't live there." As in the example presented earlier, specifically detail the incorrect items as listed in your report, describe why they are incorrect and provide supporting documentation. In our example, proof of identity and verification of the mailing address was provided in the form of enclosures included with the dispute letter.

Keep this in mind when later disputing negative account entries detailed in your credit reports. Submitting several disputes in a single correspondence would likely cause your disputes to be flagged as "frivolous". Hence, I prefer to submit them individually.

If you are curious about why I devoted time to the topic of securing your personal information, here is the answer. I do not have details about how

---

[5] https://www.ftc.gov/system/files/documents/statutes/fair-credit-reporting-act/545a_fair-credit-reporting-act-0918.pdf

these credit reporting companies verify personal information connected to each account. But it would certainly appear frivolous to file a dispute claiming an address is not yours when a quick search of a people finder site shows otherwise.

Before filing any disputes, please clean up any erroneous personal information. Also, removing your personal details from easy public access quicky adds one more layer of protection from identity theft and credit fraud.

Using the Dispute Process

We have already looked at the laws that allow you to dispute items on your credit reports. Hopefully you have used the process to delete any false personal information, from which you should receive responses in two to three weeks.

Filing valid disputes and receiving timely results does not always go smoothly. This section pinpoints critical details spelled out within the legal requirements for credit report disputes. You will learn how to use them to your advantage for best results. Also, we will highlight common tricks the credit reporting companies use to confuse consumers during the process so you can identify and avoid them.

When submitting disputes in general, I try to pretend I am the one who will receive the letter and process it. If I open an envelope and see what looks like thirty items copied and pasted that someone claims should be disputed right away, I think would call it frivolous and toss it aside. With that in mind, I have also considered advice I have read from others who say not to dispute more than nine or ten items at one time.

I have my own suggestion, which has worked well for me. How many items do I dispute in each correspondence? Exactly one. This does not mean that I only submit a single dispute and wait for the results. I have filed four disputes on the same day, but they were detailed in separate documents and mailed individually.

Whichever individuals receive my disputes will process them independent of each other. I have a reasonable expectation that more undivided attention will be afforded to a dispute when it is the sole focus of a correspondence. I can also track the dates I mailed them, record when the disputes were received and track when to expect responses more easily after submitting them individually. This strategy is perhaps just a matter of personal preference, so I do not discount any contrary advice you might have seen elsewhere.

Additionally, every dispute correspondence should be sent as certified mail – I recommend paying extra for a receipt to be returned to you upon delivery, even as it nearly doubles the cost. Why? Because, despite random advice I have read concerning backdating dispute letters to reduce time the companies have to process them, the FCRA has one specific requirement.

Once again, as detailed in the FCRA, the time limit for reinvestigation of a dispute is as follows:

§ 611. Procedure in case of disputed accuracy [15 U.S.C. § 1681i]

(a) Reinvestigations of Disputed Information

    (1) Reinvestigation Required

        (A) In general. Subject to subsection (f), and except as provided in subsection (g) if the completeness or accuracy of any item of information contained in a consumer's file at a consumer reporting agency is disputed by the consumer and the consumer notifies the agency directly, or indirectly through a reseller, of such dispute, the agency shall, free of charge, conduct a reasonable reinvestigation to determine whether the disputed information is inaccurate and record the current status of the disputed information, or delete the item from the file in accordance with paragraph (5), before the end of the 30-day period beginning on the date on which the agency receives the notice of the dispute from the consumer or reseller.

You can see the legal time limit of 30 days begins on the date in which the agency receives the notice of the dispute. For this reason, certified mail should be the method for sending your dispute letters and always purchase the return receipt request. The date on each of the delivery receipt will represent the definitive start to each 30-day period.

Perhaps you have already created logins to access your credit reports at Equifax, Experian and TransUnion using their websites. If you did, you might have seen links that read "dispute this" for "file a dispute online". *Never dispute anything using a website* except trivial details of your personal information.

Companies like to use telephones and email and their own websites most of all. The reasons are convenience and speed. The credit reporting companies each would also prefer not to delete any of the information in their files about you. The information they collect on consumers is worth billions of dollars, so deleting any could reduce its value. Hence, if an uninformed consumer initiates a dispute on the website for Experian, they will likely receive a summary notification after a few days that reports "results are ready", with a convenient button to click to access them.

What is really happening behind the scenes is the credit reporting company is using one loophole in the FCRA, which is specifically allowed, to satisfy their legal reporting requirements. We have seen that section 609, Disclosures to consumers [15 U.S.C. § 1681g] entitles each of us (consumers) to be given the information in our credit files including the sources of the information. But read carefully what is detailed in the overlooked section 610:

§ 610. Conditions and form of disclosure to consumers [15 U.S.C. § 1681h]

(a) In General

(1) *Proper identification.* A consumer reporting agency shall require, as a condition of making the disclosures required under section 609 [§ 1681g], that the consumer furnish proper identification.

(2) *Disclosure in writing.* Except as provided in subsection (b), the disclosures required to be made under section 609 [§ 1681g] shall be provided under that section in writing.

(b) Other Forms of Disclosure

(1) *In general.* If authorized by a consumer, a consumer reporting agency may make the disclosures required under 609 [§ 1681g]

(A) other than in writing; and

(B) in such form as may be

(i) specified by the consumer in accordance with paragraph (2); and

(ii) available from the agency.

(2) *Form.* A consumer may specify pursuant to paragraph (1) that disclosures under section 609 [§ 1681g] shall be made

(A) in person, upon the appearance of the consumer at the place of business of the consumer reporting agency where disclosures are regularly provided, during normal business hours, and on reasonable notice;

(B) by telephone, if the consumer has made a written request for disclosure by telephone;

(C) by electronic means, if available from the agency; or

(D) by any other reasonable means that is available from the agency.

(c) *Trained personnel.* Any consumer reporting agency shall provide trained personnel to explain to the consumer any information furnished to him pursuant to section 609 [§ 1681g] of this title.

(d) *Persons accompanying consumer.* The consumer shall be permitted to be accompanied by one other person of his choosing, who shall furnish reasonable identification. A consumer reporting agency may require the consumer to furnish a written statement granting permission to the consumer reporting agency to discuss the consumer's file in such person's presence.

(e) *Limitation of liability.* Except as provided in sections 616 and 617 [§§ 1681n and 1681o] of this title, no consumer may bring any action or proceeding in the nature of defamation, invasion of privacy, or negligence with respect to the reporting of information against any consumer reporting agency, any user of information, or any person who furnishes information to a consumer reporting agency, based on information disclosed pursuant to section 609, 610, or 615 [§§ 1681g, 1681h, or 1681m] of this title or based on information disclosed by a user of a consumer report to or for a consumer against whom the user has taken adverse action, based in whole or in part on the report, except as to false information furnished with malice or willful intent to injure such consumer.

Overall, section 610 of the FCRA guarantees that once we have supplied proper identifying documentation, the credit reporting companies must provide requested information to each of us *in writing*, unless we authorize them to disclose it in methods other than in writing. Before filing an online dispute with either of the three credit reporting companies online, carefully read their terms of service, because that is exactly what you are doing.

Why am I so hung up on having everything documented and on paper? Aren't email and websites way faster? They certainly are, and that is precisely why I do not use them when disputing items on my credit reports.

Time is required for a person to create a written response to your dispute, and to also provide the method of verification they used to determine the validity of the disputed item. Online disputes allow the credit reporting companies to sidestep these two very important tasks, which removes some of your rights guaranteed by the FCRA[6].

Once you have submitted disputes, wait for the responses and resultant actions to be mailed to you. Do not communicate with the credit reporting companies concerning your dispute again, even if just to respond to a seemingly innocent message such as "we want to verify the details of your dispute."

Thirty days is the legal time limit each company is permitted to process disputes. But if more information is received by the consumer in that time, the credit companies are allowed up to fifteen additional days. This is detailed in the FCRA:

§ 611. Procedure in case of disputed accuracy [15 U.S.C. § 1681i] (a) (1)

(B) Extension of period to reinvestigate. Except as provided in subparagraph (c), the 30-day period described in subparagraph (A) may be extended for not more than 15 additional days if the consumer reporting agency receives information from the consumer during that 30-day period that is relevant to the reinvestigation

---

[6] www.investopedia.com/avoid-these-credit-repair-mistakes-4769722

Answering even one question related to a dispute while reinvestigation is underway automatically entitles the credit reporting company to fifteen additional days for investigation. Do not communicate with a credit reporting company while an investigation is in progress.

Credit reporting companies are required to verify and validate negative information that has been added to your credit reports. This is guaranteed by law. Negative information about any of your accounts must also be substantiated to prove that it is valid. The so called 609 dispute letters, although named incorrectly, do serve a purpose.

Every dispute you file must be processed as guaranteed by Section 611 of the FCRA. As part of your dispute letters, you should also mention Section 609 which legally requires the companies to disclose all information in your file which was used to create your credit report. This is where dealing with the credit reporting companies can be tricky.

Read this excerpt from the website of Experian, concerning 609 letters[7]:

The 609 Dispute Letter theory is if you ask the credit bureaus for information they clearly cannot produce as part of your dispute letter, like the original signed copies of your

---

[7] https://www.experian.com/blogs/ask-experian/what-is-a-609-

credit applications or the cashed checks used for bill payment, then they would have to remove the disputed item because it's unverifiable. The FCRA, however, entitles us to all of the information the credit reporting agencies have in their systems—not information they do not have in their systems.

Their summary is cleverly written but misleadingly false! Yes, the FCRA specifically entitles us to all the information the credit reporting agencies have about us in their systems. But, concerning information they do not have, there is no mention in the FCRA. Why? The answer is obvious.

All entries in the credit reports must be substantiated and cannot be arbitrary. When challenged with a dispute, the company must prove that the account details are correct. If supporting information is not in their files, it must still be obtained, and they have thirty days to get it. If an account entry cannot be validated by a credit reporting company, it legally must be removed.

In summary, a dispute correspondence should not be called a 609 letter. Section 609 of the FCRA *should* be referenced when challenging the credit reporting companies about details you do not recognize or believe to be incorrect. Be vigilant when disputing negative accounts on your credit reports.

Do not expect to have complete success when you file disputes. You may have to send follow up letters. When this happens, which is likely, reference the original dates when you communicated with each agency in case the time limit has expired. If an agency claims to have verified an account you disputed but did not provide supporting details, dispute it again referencing the FCRA and require them to send copies of the source of the information to you in writing.

When follow up disputes are necessary, be sure to state that you do not authorize a response to be provided by any means other than a written response sent via mail. Reference the Section 610 (a) (2) of the FCRA, which says (in part):

> *Disclosure in writing.* Except as provided in subsection (b), the disclosures required to be made under section 609 [§ 1681g] shall be provided under that section in writing.

The remainder of section 610 details other methods of disclosure that you could authorize. By specifically stating you only authorize a written response be mailed, you add a legal constraint.

In follow-up disputes, when necessary, you should also mention that you require a copy of any signed contract or legally binding document be sent that validates the account as being yours, not just their word that they claim to have validated it.

Strong language might also be used to convey the seriousness of your dispute. Section 610 (e) of the FCRA describes how each credit reporting agency is protected from legal liability:

(e) *Limitation of liability.* Except as provided in sections 616 and 617 [§§ 1681n and 1681o] of this title, no consumer may bring any action or proceeding in the nature of defamation, invasion of privacy, or negligence with respect to the reporting of information against any consumer reporting agency, any user of information, or any person who furnishes information to a consumer reporting agency, based on information disclosed pursuant to section 609, 610, or 615 [§§ 1681g, 1681h, or 1681m] of this title or based on information disclosed by a user of a consumer report to or for a consumer against whom the user has taken adverse action, based in whole or in part on the report, except as to false information furnished with malice or willful intent to injure such consumer.

In your correspondence remind each credit reporting company that you are being injured by the negative information that has not been validated. If the negative account detail remains on your report without being validated after multiple requests, then it is willful intent so you can then sue them for liability. Quoting section 610 (e) might prove helpful.

One important thing to remember is that disputes are for removing *inaccurate* information. Do not expect success removing valid negative accounts from your credit reports by filing disputes.

Building Good Credit

Once you have reviewed your credit reports, you will know exactly what impacted them in the past. You should next focus on your actions today that will build better credit going forward.

I will describe what I had been doing wrong until very recently concerning my own credit situation. I already ran into problems in the past, so I was determined to better manage my credit. I made sure that I kept low balances on all five of my credit cards, and rarely used them. I installed a calendar app on my phone to remind me about the due dates, so I always made the payments on time. And I paid at least five dollars more than the minimum payments every month, to build a good credit history.

I was smart enough to know that interest payments are bad for personal finances, especially the high rates lenders charge people with bad credit. I normally made purchases using my debit card since it was just like using cash. This way I could keep my credit utilization low. After a few months of following those rules, my credit should have improved. And the banks could have seen how responsible I was with the credit they extended me on their cards so they would likely increase my credit limits.

Or so I thought.

Now I will share what I learned so you can avoid making the mistakes I did. Everything starts with the most basic question. What is credit? Credit, in a nutshell, means using other people's money. If something involves the use of credit it involves the use of other people's money. Your credit history is the history of what has happened after you used other people's money. Two types of credit are installment accounts and revolving accounts.

Installment accounts, like mortgages and personal loans, involve a debt agreed upon in advance, that requires scheduled payments until the entire debt is satisfied. The debt typically includes fees and interest, which is how the lenders benefit from the arrangement. Payments are typically made in monthly installments.

Revolving accounts, which are most popularly reported to the credit bureaus, are basically never ending. Creditors allow you to spend up to a maximum amount of their money, which is called your credit limit. Unlike installment accounts however, as you make payments to reduce the debt, you can immediately spend more of the creditor's money until you reach your credit limit again. This revolving circle of debt is why they are called revolving accounts. And yes, revolving accounts also include fees and interest, which benefit the lenders tremendously.

Much more is reported about revolving accounts than I first thought, which was the amount of each payment and whether they were made on time. Companies track the maximum balances during each billing cycle, average daily balances, and the ratios of credit used to total available credit. Several additional details paint a more complete, and unfortunately a less favorable picture than what I once believed.

Correctly using credit cards and making credit building payments involves a few key dates. Every month the credit card issuers will send you a statement summarizing the purchases and payments made during the most recent period. Each period, known as the billing cycle, begins immediately after the previous one. Every billing cycle, as detailed in the monthly bill, ends on the statement closing date.

Never pay a credit card bill after its due date because late fees could be charged, in addition to having a negative detail added to your credit reports. But simply making timely payments is not enough. The trick is to focus attention on the statement closing date.

The account balance on an account's statement closing date is what is included in credit report updates. The importance of this can be illustrated with an example.

Consider a credit card that has a limit of $300. The cardholder makes purchases totaling $270, so they have reached 90% utilization (they have used 90 percent of their credit limit on the account). When they get their bill and read the due date, the cardholder decides to pay the full balance a week early. The cardholder repeats this each month, but when checking their credit score with a free app their account continues to report high utilization. The cardholder knows that something must be wrong since they pay the account down to a near zero balance before every due date. What is going on?

Behind the scenes, here is what is happening. The cardholder makes purchases with their credit card, and on the statement closing date, which ends the billing cycle, the credit card issuer reports the account balance to the credit agencies. Although the due date is actually weeks later, this balance on the statement closing date is reported. So, when the customer pays the bill each month, even in full, the account always has high utilization as far as the credit reporting companies are concerned.

A simple change to the way the cardholder handles the account would make a huge difference. Without using the card any less, the customer could note the statement closing date on their calendar – an old-fashioned physical calendar, printed on paper. The billing cycle should be detailed on the credit card statement, but a quick call to the card issuer will confirm the date.

By making a payment in time to have the balance be zero (or below 10% of the limit as some recommend) by the statement closing date, the issuer will report a nearly zero balance to the credit reporting companies every month. The cardholder can continue using the card as normal after the statement closing date, because the low or zero balance will have already been reported. When using this technique, keep in mind that credit issuers like Capital One sometimes report the account balance up to four days after the actual statement closing date, so it is a good idea to avoid new purchases during that short window just in case.

Changing your payments to accommodate the statement closing dates is one action that will greatly improve your credit. Another is changing the amount of spending you do with your credit cards. If you spend a lot of cash, or use debit cards, consider modifying the way you spend your money.

Responsible credit use means you regularly demonstrate the responsible use of other people's money. When you use a debit card or pay with cash you only show that you can spend your own money. Credit always entails using other people's money. If you have bad credit and low credit limits, reporting low utilization to the credit reporting companies is just one part of the puzzle. Another is demonstrating to the creditors that you can actually use significant amounts of their money and quickly pay it back. You can do this without putting yourself further in debt.

Every month there are usually some things that you pay for with cash or by using a card that debits your bank account. Changing your method of spending for these items will help build your credit without spending any more than you already do. Before you purchase something, make a note of the cost. Set aside the cash you would have spent, then charge it to your credit card instead. Before your statement closing date, which you will readily see on your calendar, use the cash you have allocated and pay your credit card bill(s) the total sum. Develop a habit of using this method.

What you will accomplish by using this method is demonstrating responsible credit use. Without increasing the amount of money that you would have ordinarily spent your creditors will see your new pattern of using other people's money. Your creditors will also report your account(s) to Equifax, Experian and TransUnion showing a near zero balance and very low credit utilization. This positive account status will be added to your credit reports.

There is an important additional benefit to using this credit building method. Aside from more positive history at the credit reporting companies, you will build more credit with your actual creditors. Here is another behind the scenes insight. Creditors prefer to keep you in debt.

Finance charges increase the debt you owe the creditors when you carry a balance from one billing cycle to the next. If you utilize the spending method we illustrated earlier, you will avoid practically all finance charges – and the card issuer will make practically no money from you. Creditors rely upon keeping you in debt to earn their billions.

By repeatedly demonstrating that you can approach your spending limit each month but pay it off in full (without incurring finance charges), your creditors will take notice. Within about six months each will likely offer you credit limit increases. Do not mistake this for being a congratulatory award.

Credit limit increases are a tactic your creditors employ to push the envelope, hoping to tip the scales of debt in their favor. By increasing the credit limit on your accounts, creditors gamble that you might increase your spending and exceed the amount you are able to quickly pay back. If you are enticed by higher limits and increase your credit usage, you might carry a balance beyond one billing cycle. Then the creditors could finally profit from the finance charges.

After earning credit increases, do not fall into the trap that has been set for you. Simply adjust your spending if you have multiple credit cards, to bring just one closer to its limit and pay it off that cycle, then alternate between each of the others. Do not exceed your normal spending patterns and risk being unable to settle each balance within the single billing cycle. Tracking billing cycles, balances and managing accounts this way is part of what has been nicknamed "the credit game."

Moving from poor credit scores to good credit requires consistent effort and this does not happen overnight. We have given you the foundation to get you started, and you can find more complex topics with simple internet searches. Mastering credit is a lot like writing a publication. You want the punctuation to be just right, and have it convey exactly the message you intended. With practice, regular effort, and time, you will add positive credit history and have better credit scores.

Do you still think you should hire a credit repair company to fix your credit?

Use this book as a starting point. Remember that credit scores are a continuing reflection of your financial history. Develop habits that result in gaining higher credit scores and you will put yourself in a better position financially.

There are some things in life that you must do for yourself.

Appendix

Credit reporting company mailing addresses:

Equifax Information Services LLC
P.O. Box 740256
Atlanta, GA 30374-0256

Experian
P.O. Box 4500
Allen, TX 75013

TransUnion LLC
Consumer Dispute Center
P.O. Box 2000
Chester, PA 19016